First World War
and Army of Occupation
War Diary
France, Belgium and Germany

60 DIVISION
Divisional Troops
Royal Army Medical Corps
2/4 London Field Ambulance
1 September 1915 - 31 December 1915

WO95/3029/1-2

The Naval & Military Press Ltd
www.nmarchive.com
Published in association with The National Archives

Published by

The Naval & Military Press Ltd

Unit 10 Ridgewood Industrial Park,

Uckfield, East Sussex,

TN22 5QE England

Tel: +44 (0) 1825 749494

www.naval-military-press.com

www.nmarchive.com

This diary has been reprinted in facsimile from the original. Any imperfections are inevitably reproduced and the quality may fall short of modern type and cartographic standards.

© Crown Copyright
Images reproduced by permission of The National Archives, London, England, 2015.

Contents

Document type	Place/Title	Date From	Date To
Heading	WO95/3029 1915 June-1916		
Heading	60th Division 2-4th London Fld Amb. 1915 Sep-1915 Dec And 1916 Jun-1916 Nov		
Heading	WO95/3029/1		
Miscellaneous	Report Attached To War Diary For August	02/09/1915	02/09/1915
War Diary	Saffron Walden	01/09/1915	30/09/1915
Miscellaneous	Saffron Walden	04/10/1915	04/10/1915
War Diary	Bishops Stortford	01/10/1915	30/11/1915
Operation(al) Order(s)	179th Infantry Brigade Operation Orders No. 1	04/11/1915	04/11/1915
Miscellaneous	Ref 11. G Ord Map 29		
Miscellaneous	E.b 409	03/12/1915	03/12/1915
War Diary	Saffron Walden	01/10/1915	05/10/1915
War Diary	Stebbing	05/10/1915	06/10/1915
War Diary	Braintree	07/10/1915	08/10/1915
War Diary	Saffron Walden	11/10/1915	14/10/1915
War Diary	Ort-Ord HQ	15/10/1915	15/10/1915
War Diary	Saffron Walden	18/10/1915	19/10/1915
War Diary	Stebbing	20/10/1915	20/10/1915
War Diary	Braintree	21/10/1915	21/10/1915
War Diary	Stebbing	22/10/1915	22/10/1915
War Diary	Saffron Walden	23/10/1915	26/10/1915
War Diary	Bishops Stortford	27/10/1915	31/10/1915
Heading	War Diary of the 2/4th London Field Ambulance From 1st December 1915 To 31st December 1915 Volume 12		
War Diary	Bishops Stortford	01/12/1915	31/12/1915
Miscellaneous	Report On Field Ambulance Reception Hospital For Period Nov 4th-Dec 16th 1915	16/12/1915	16/12/1915
Heading	2/4 London Field Ambulance War Diary Oct 1915 Appendix I		
Miscellaneous	A Form Messages And Signals		
Miscellaneous	The Above Arrangement Proved Satisfactory & Ran A Smoothly After The Past For Days		
Miscellaneous	The Change Of The Hospital		
Miscellaneous	Report Of M.Q. i/c Reception Hospital	31/12/1915	31/12/1915

WO 95

3029

1915 June – 1916 Nov.
file
check Nov 1915

60TH DIVISION

2-4TH LONDON FLD AMB.

~~JUN - NOV 1916~~

1915 SEP - 1915 DEC
AND
1916 JUN - 1916 NOV

WO 95/3029/1

3/4. London Field Ambulance
Saffron Walden
2.IX.15.

Report attached to war diary for August

Training.

During the month less field work has been done than usual. Such as has been done has been elementary work on the collection of wounded. A draft of 30 men from the 3/4 London Field Ambulance has been received, and their training has been used to see whether these men knew anything about their work. Generally speaking their work is good, and they seem to be a good set of men.

In addition 30 recruits have joined, and they have been kept at their recruit drill.

Some considerable time has been spent in teaching the men how to settle down into camp, and lectures have been given on camp sanitation exemplified by the arrangements in the camp.

Discipline.

In continuation of last month's report, I have noticed a very considerable improvement in the discipline of the unit, in excess even of what I had hoped. I am still far from satisfied with the way in which the interior economy of the unit works, the general routine does not seem to work nearly so smoothly as in the battalions of the 179th (London) Infantry Brigade.

T B Layton
Major
O.C. 3/4 London Field Ambulance

WAR DIARY 2/1 London Field Ambulance

INTELLIGENCE SUMMARY — SEPTEMBER

Army Form C. 2118.

Hour, Date, Place	Summary of Events and Information	Remarks and references to Appendices
SAFFRON WALDEN 1.IX.15	Transport and detachment of 100 men sent out on Brigade Convoy scheme under Lieut SPENCER. Being unaccustomed to units arrived at the finish, about half this end of the convoy was test-race. T.B.L.	
2.IX.15	Inspection of Transport by O.C. 179th (London) Infantry Brigade. one ambulance wagon, and curtain wagon, ordered cast off. Muster role paid in parade. T.B.L.	
3.IX.15	Practice for classes. Y.R.L.	
4.IX.15	Instructor's collection of wounded. T.B.L.	
6.IX.15	Preparation for classes. Y.R.L.	
	Lect. b. W.B. resuscitation — heatstroke. T.B.L.	
7.IX.15	Field day near Little Chesterford. T.B.L.	
8.IX.15	Turning our Equipment. T.B.L.	
	Field work under Capt NASH 2/1 ASHDON. T.B.L.	
9.IX.15 11:30pm	A Zeppelin passed over the camp, without disturbance. T.B.L.	
9.IX.15	Turning our equipment — avoiding sparks — Sing Song. T.B.L.	
10.IX.15	March behind 2/Battalion (LITTLEBURY) 2/R.L.	
	Night work — collection of wounded.	
13.9.15	Practice of (Removing Wounded) from trenches. T.B.L.	
14.9.15	Dressing Station exercise — Head Staff. Y.B.L.	
15.9.15	Instruction — collection of wounded Y.R.L.	
16.9.15	Transport wagons on trunk of Ashdown T.B.L.	
	Inspected Transport by O.C. 60 London Div Field Amb. T.B.L.	

WAR DIARY
or
INTELLIGENCE SUMMARY.

1/1 London Field Amb/ce SEPTEMBER.

Army Form C. 2118.

(Erase heading not required.)

Hour, Date, Place	Summary of Events and Information	Remarks and references to Appendices
17.9.15.	Loading wagons on trucks at Theeton. TRL.	
20.9.15.	Removal of wounded from Trenches TRL.	
22.9.15.	Preparation for move. TRL.	
23.9.15.	Practice alarm — unit moved to QUENDON — Inspection by G.O.C. 60th (London) Division TRL.	
27–28.9.15.	Projected Tactical Scheme — HEYDON – CHRISHALL. TRL. Field Ambulance in Bivouac at ELMDON. TRL.	
30.9.15.	Trg all day. unit moved. STUMPS CROSS – LINTON. HADSTOCK. TRL.	

T.W.Cuyler

Saffron Walden
4.X.15.

During the month of September the discipline and administration of the unit has greatly improved.

The presence of a transport officer has been of the greatest assistance. Lieut Lambert is as yet not very good on parade, but is most excellent in the Horse lines, and has a complete knowledge of wagons, horses and harness.

There is unfortunately a feeling rife among officers, N.C.O's and men that no more Territorial Troops are going abroad and that we are to be used only for home defence. This results in many wanting to transfer.

J B Langh
Major
o. c. 2/4 London Fd W Amb

Feb 1915 98 E

WAR DIARY 2/1 London Field Ambulance Army Form C. 2118.
or
INTELLIGENCE SUMMARY.
(Erase heading not required.)

Rafed Survey
1/2 in = 1 mile
Sheet 29.

Hour, Date, Place	Summary of Events and Information	Remarks and references to Appendices
BISHOPS STORTFORD 1.V.15	Compy duties 7/3L.	
2.V.15	Compy duties 7/3L.	
3.V.15	Fd Ambulance did field operations with Capt NASH 7/3L at BURY GREEN & GREEN TYE. O.C. structors attend MS officer rendered arrangements for opening orders etc. see appx I	See appx I
	Brigade scheme — opened orders etc. 7/3L	
4.V.15	Squad drill — lecture by Capt NASH — Resuscitation 7/3L	
5.V.15	afternoon — 3 sections in bandaging etc. — 40 men to R.C.S.	7/3L
	Lecture by Pvt KEITH	
6.V.15	Saturday — general duties — half holiday 7/3L	
7.V.15	Church parade 7/3L	
8.V.15	Field ambulance drill in field on MUCH HADHAM Road 7/3L	
	Lecture to officers by G.O.C. 7/3L	
9.V.15	Inspection by A.D.M.S.	7/3L
	Lecture in bandaging in afternoon	
10.V.15	Fieldwork — squad worked along Road to Widmouth E & of	
	D. in MAGGOTS END — march across country to Road	

P.T.O.

WAR DIARY
Nicholson Pr.B.Caul

or

INTELLIGENCE SUMMARY.
(Erase heading not required.)

Army Form C. 2118.

Hour, Date, Place	Summary of Events and Information	Remarks and references to Appendices
BISHOPS STORTFORD		
10.x.15. (cont'd)	S. of point 342. E. of FURNEAUX PELHAM. Fairly well done – one squad (started) lost. T.P.L.	
11.x.15.	Book inspection – and two out of ford. Lecture on advancing by Coy. Fieldwork under Capt. NASH at GT. HALLINGBURY. Discussion on map reading with N.C.Os. & proprietors Coy. T.P.L. and No 2 beans & pen.	
12.x.15.	Pouring with rain. Lectures morning & afternoon. T.P.L.	
14.x.15.	28 fatigue cases – Church parade – C.O. & T.O. practising and country work – Inspection of boots by major HAWORTH. T.P.L. Fine cold – fieldwork under Capt. NASH – cross country from MUCH HADHAM to MORLEY. T.P.L.	
15.x.15.		
16.x.15.	Snow covered ground – battles to fall with umpires use – Lecture by C.O. in morning and march & maneuvre Plan Class in afternoon. T.P.L.	
17.x.15.	Foggy. Coy.St.Dennis – needs like glass – field work near TAKELEY. T.P.L.	

6/1915
Palmerston Aubitaule R.F.A.
Army Form C. 2118.

WAR DIARY
or
INTELLIGENCE SUMMARY.
(Erase heading not required.)

Instructions regarding War Diaries and Intelligence Summaries are contained in F. S. Regs., Part II. and the Staff Manual respectively. Title pages will be prepared in manuscript.

Hour, Date, Place	Summary of Events and Information	Remarks and references to Appendices

18. XI. 15. — Raining all day — Lecture on Manufacture by Capt PRICE HARRIS in the evening — route march in the afternoon — Fatigues JR.

19. XI. 15. — Fatigues — Lecture by Capt NASH. 78.L.

20. XI. 15. — Physical Drill — pay JR.

21. XI. 15. — Church Parade JR.

22. XI. 15. — Wet work with Capt NASH at ALBURY LODGE — leave of absence every hour JRL.

23. XI. 15. — Lecture by C.O. — physical drill — entraining practice 7RL.

24. XI. 15. — Fieldwork at BIRCHANGER — inspection 7RL.

25. XI. 15. — Second case of mumps — lecture by Capt PRITCHARD — work in march JRL.

26. XI. 15. — Personal & company drill — lecture by C.O. — lecture attended by C. Rev. Vd. — entraining practice 7RL.

27. XI. 15. — Fatigues JRL — pay etc. JRL.

28. XI. 15. — Fatigues — Church parade 78.L.

Oct 1915. Pg iv

Army Form C. 2118.

WAR DIARY
or
INTELLIGENCE SUMMARY.
(Erase heading not required.)

Instructions regarding War Diaries and Intelligence Summaries are contained in F.S. Regs., Part II. and the Staff Manual respectively. Title pages will be prepared in manuscript.

Hour, Date, Place	Summary of Events and Information	Remarks and references to Appendices
29.XI.15.	Trooping early followed by march & field exits — THORLEY HOUSES — practice cocures — country wandering by Maps — and ry road — C₄ TRIMS GREEN — generally very brilliant day.	
30.XI.15.	Physical Drill — Lectures by Co. — no training — 7th Aid Class — Lectures on war-readiness with PRs. TBL.	

179th Infantry Brigade.

OPERATION ORDERS NO. 1.

Copy No. 8.

Wind Hill
Bishop's Stortford.
November 4th 1915.

Ref.Map:
O.S.Sheet 29.
1" = 1 Mile.

INFORMATION. 1. A White Force is advancing from Cambridge on London. The Advanced Guard strength about one Brigade with Artillery, reached Saffron Walden on the night of November 3rd 1915.

INTENTION. 2. The O.C., 179th Brigade intends to push on towards Quendon and prevent the Enemy advancing.

STARTING POINT. 3. The Starting Point will be Road Junction EAST of WICKHAM HALL on Bishop's Stortford – Stansted Road.

ADVANCED GUARD. 4.
Comdg. Lt.Col.E.F.Strange,
2/15th Battn.
1 Platoon 60th Lon.Dvn.Cyclist Co.
1 Batty.2/7th Bde.R.F.A.
2/15th Battalion.

The Advanced Guard, as per margin, will march via STANSTED – QUENDON and discover the position and strength of the Enemy, and will endeavour to destroy the Railway Bridges at NEWPORT and N. of QUENDON.

MAIN BODY. 5.
No.2 Sec.Signal Co.
2/16th Battalion.
2/7th Brigade R.F.A.
 less 1 Batty.
2/14th Battalion.
 less 1 Platoon.

The Main Body will pass the Starting Point at 9.30 a.m. and follow the Advanced Guard.

REAR GUARD. 6.
1 Co. 2/14th Battalion.
 less 3 Platoons.

The Rear Guard will follow ½ mile in rear of the main body.

MEDICAL. 7. The 2/4th Field Ambulance will follow the Main Body three miles in Rear.

AMMUNITION 8. 100 Rounds per man will be carried in the Regimental Reserve.

BRIGADE AMMUNITION RESERVE. 9. Each Unit will detail 2 S.A.A. Carts and furnish the Brigade Ammunition Reserve, which will march in rear of the Main Body.
O.C., 2/16th Battalion will detail an Officer to be in charge of Brigade Ammunition Reserve: Also one N.C.O. and two Orderlies to deal with requisitions.

REPORTS. 10. Reports to Head of Main Column.

BY ORDER,
B. LEVETT.
Captain & Brigade Major.
179th Infantry Brigade.

Issued at 7.30 a.m.
No. 1. Operation Orders File.
 2. War Diary.
 3. G.O.C., 60th (Lon) Division.
 4. O.C., 2/7th Bde. R.F.A.
 5. O.C., 2/14th Battalion.
 6. O.C., 2/15th Battalion.
 7. O.C., 2/16th Battalion.
 8. O.C., 2/4th Field Ambulance.
 9. O.C., 60th (Lon) Divl.Cyclist Co.
 10. O.C., No.2 Sec.Divl.Signal Co.

- 2 -

NOTES.

1. The 2/7th Brigade R.F.A., will join the Advanced Guard and Main Body at Stansted.

2. No Troops will move W. of the line CLAVERING - BERDON - UPEND - FARNHAM GREEN or E. of the Line DEBDEN - HAMPERDON END - 2nd C. in CHICKNEY.

3. The White Force will wear White Bands in the Caps.

Ref H G
6 May 29.
at 11.23 am 8/15 mins
received a check
at road fork W J
FOREST HALL
giving to 2/6 Anthem
coming up road
BISHOP STORTFORD
— QUENDON
WEST of RAILWAY

3. XII. 15

E.B. 209.

Training during the past month has been devoted to Medical & Surgical first aid, and on the Field work largely to map reading.

Two cases of mange among the horses has necessitated the complete disinfection of stables and horses, and has interfered with the field training of the Transport details.

A system of dealing with scabies & pediculosis has been organised at the cleansing station. This is affording a valuable training to the nursing orderlies and officers.

No night work has been done, I hope to begin this again shortly.

Discipline in billets has been good shewing a marked improvement on the time when we were formerly in billets.

The lecture on discipline by the G.O.C. has been of great help to me in improving the discipline among officers & N.C.Os.

T. B. Layton   Major
O.C. 2/1 London Field Ambulance

Army Form C. 2118.

2/1 London Fd Ambulance
October

WAR DIARY
or
INTELLIGENCE SUMMARY.
(Erase heading not required.)

Instructions regarding War Diaries and Intelligence Summaries are contained in F.S. Regs., Part II. and the Staff Manual respectively. Title pages will be prepared in manuscript.

Hour, Date, Place	Summary of Events and Information	Remarks and references to Appendices
SAFFRON WALDEN 1.X.15.	Drill of Field Ambulance with wagons. JRC	
do 2.X.15.	Paraded in Gas-to-battle, inspecting & homeward. JRC	
do 3.X.15.	Wagons loaded ready to move. JRC	
do 5.X.15.	Route march with Brigade to STEBBING. JRC	
STEBBING 5.X.15. 2.15pm	arrived THRDES from 2.15pm. JRC day attacked. Receiving wounded - Dressing Receiving station set up. JRC	For details see app. I already sent in.
do 6.X.15.	Woken night "some rain - advanced" reinf 178th R.B. IE - dressing station opened at Farm with JHQ in ROMAN ROAD at Spain Hall S.H.W in WORKHOUSE. JRC Bivouacked for night at Farm. JRC Retirement of Field Station - Field Amb. returned to BRAINTREE. JRC	
BRAINTREE 7.X.15.	THRDES - Return to SAFFRON WALDEN. JRC	
8.X.15.		
SAFFRON WALDEN 9.X.15.	Camp duties JRC	
11.X.15.	do do JRC	
12.X.15.	do do JRC	
13.X.15.	Fd Ambulance servant off in Aug & 8th Divisional	App.R.No 2 (already sent in)
14.X.15.	entrainment at MANUDEN - Divisional Station Staff up at ORFORD HOUSE JRC	

WAR DIARY
or
INTELLIGENCE SUMMARY.
(Erase heading not required.)

Army Form C. 2118.

Hour, Date, Place	Summary of Events and Information	Remarks and references to Appendices
ORFORD HO 15.X.15	returned to Saffron Walden M.L	
SAFFRON WALDEN 18.X.15	Camp duties M.L	
19.X.15	marched to Thaxted M.L	
STEBBING 21.X.15	Force engagement - Divisional Statur at Makers Farm M.L with blue army	
BRAINTREE 21.X.15	6.X.15 M.L	
STEBBING 22.X.15	return to Stebbing M.L	
SAFFRON WALDEN 23.X.15	return to Saffron Walden M.L	
25.X.15	camp duties M.L	
26.X.15	transport tent stores to Stortford M.L	
BISHOPS STORTFORD 27.X.15	Route march to Stortford M.L	
28.X.15	settling down into billets M.L	M.L
29.X.15	do do do do	M.L
30.X.15	do do do do	M.L
31.X.15	do do do do	M.L

CONFIDENTIAL.

WAR DIARY of the
2/4th LONDON FIELD AMBULANCE.

From 1st DECEMBER 1915 to 31st DECEMBER 1915

VOLUME 12.

WAR DIARY
or
INTELLIGENCE SUMMARY.
(Erase heading not required.)

Army Form C. 2118.

Hour, Date, Place	Summary of Events and Information	Remarks and references to Appendices
BISHOPS STORTFORD 1.XII.15	Pouring with rain - route march O.C. Lt HALLINGBURY 712.	
2.XII.15	Misty day - Physical drill - lecture by Capt PRICE HARRIS. Route march in afternoon - map reading class in evening 712.	
3.XII.15	Raining Day - lecture by Capt SPENCER - 40 men to R.C. Surgeon in afternoon 712.	
4.XII.15	Pouring with rain - admin to the orderly 712.	
5.XII.15	Fire in Evening - church parade - raining in afternoon 712.	
6.XII.15	Capt NASH detached to 2/14 H. Batt'y Pouring in the rain - Chapel 10am - route march early Capt SPENCER - Transport under T.O. - Fire day letter 712.	
7.XII.15	Fine Day in morning - heavy rain in afternoon Physical drill - lecture by Capt SPENCER	
8.XII.15	Route march in afternoon - instruction in operative surgery. 712. 3 officers to Grey's between TAKELEY and STANSTEAD Hall Fine day - Forward of 60th Division home performers by 2.PM Medical change of ZBT. ambulance - lecture by Capt PRITCHARD - inspection of hospital Railway	
9.XII.15	Wet day - lecture by Capt PRITCHARD - inspection of hospital Railway astins bathing 712.	

Army Form C. 2118.

WAR DIARY
or
INTELLIGENCE SUMMARY.
(Erase heading not required.)

Instructions regarding War Diaries and Intelligence Summaries are contained in F.S. Regs., Part II and the Staff Manual respectively. Title pages will be prepared in manuscript.

Hour, Date, Place	Summary of Events and Information	Remarks and references to Appendices
10. XII. 15.	Fine Day – Physical Drill – Lecture by C.O. – 68 men to Ref. in afternoon – rest in fatigue to wearing fields – very weak condition of ground – large tent swelled unpleasant attempt in afternoon.	JRL
11. XII. 15.	Fine Day – Training usual day – wearing fields very bad – attempts to transport it with chestnuts etc. –	JRL
12. XII. 15.	Frosty & Fine – church parade – huts in fields Trumbull aired.	JRL
13. XII. 15.	Fine Frosty – Inspection of General Hosp. by C.O. – Capt. SPENCER Ill with myalgia – Field park under Capt. RICHARRIS at EISENHAM – Brown fingering into behind wall.	JRL
14. XII. 15.	Fine weather changing to rain later – Physical drill – Lecture by C.O. – Read clever by Capt. SPENCER – 3 officers f London for auction – surfing – practice in Conham Wapeninbain(?) G.S. as medical stores ant.	JRL
15. XII. 15.	rainy day – Lecture by Capt. SPENCER – stretcher drill in YMCA hall – short front march.	JRL
16. XII. 15.	Board on equipment – physical Drill – squad & all rank march.	JRL
17. XII. 15.	Board on equipment.	JRL

Army Form C. 2118.

WAR DIARY
or
INTELLIGENCE SUMMARY.
(Erase heading not required.)

Instructions regarding War Diaries and Intelligence Summaries are contained in F.S. Regs., Part II and the Staff Manual respectively. Title pages will be prepared in manuscript.

Hour, Date, Place	Summary of Events and Information	Remarks and references to Appendices
BISHOPS STOTFORD		
18. XII. 15.	Board on Equipment - Pay - Rawkbusby Buy MK.	
19. XII. 15.	Sunday - Free day - Church parade - Broughton Equipment 7BL.	
20. XII. 15.	dusty & rainy - C/O: Board on equipment - rout march under Sergt. Major 7BL.	
21. XII. 15.	raining - wrong - Board on equipment - inspection of all kit & billets - 7BL	
22. XII. 15.	inspection of transport by OC 60th Divisional Train - Board on equipment TBL - Boarding equipment 7BL	
23. XII. 15.	Board on equipment - fatigue parties TBL. preventing to Harbury air - fatigue parties TBL.	
24. XII. 15.	Into work under Capt PRITCHARD at MUCH HADHAM 7BL.	
	OC to BUNTINGFORD & Standon 7BL	
26. XII. 15.	Christmas Day - Tea and cake - kind wermph 7BL. reconstructing parades - Church parade. 7BL.	
27. XII. 15.	Holiday. 7BL.	
28. XII. 15.	Inspection by GOC 60th (London) Division - Christmas dinner arrangement for whitewash 7BL.	
	5pm returned unstinting and flannery 7BL.	Appendix
29. XII. 15.	fatigue parties 7BL.	Sheets report of
30. XII. 15.		M.O's I/C Hospital 7BL.
31. XII. 15.	Forward under Capt PRICE HARRIS - FARNHAM 7BL.	

War Diary Dec 1915
Appendix

2/4 London Field Ambulance
R.A.M.C.T.
Bishops Stortford

Report on Field Ambulance Reception Hospital
for period Nov. 4th – Dec 16th 1915.

Medical   This Hospital was opened on Nov. 4th 1915 for the treatment of all cases of notifiable disease, including "tonsilitis", with the exception of cases diagnosed directly as diphtheria & scarlet fever which were sent to the Civil Infectious Hospitals at Bishops Stortford or Hertford & Ware joint, direct; being passed through the A & D Book.

Cases of Gonorrhoea were also passed through the A & D book & sent direct to 1st Eastern General Hospital Cambridge or Rochester Row; and any cases of Cerebro Spinal meningitis were to be passed to the 1st Eastern General Hospital if they occurred.

The Units treated at this Hospital are
179th Infantry Brigade & H.Q.
60th (Lond) Divisional Troops & H.Q.
3rd Army Troops. & H.Q.

From Nov. 4th – Nov 10th cases of general disease were admitted as no notifiable cases had occurred, & cases at this time could not be admitted to the 60th (Lond) Casualty Clearing Station.

On Nov 6th a case having been admitted as tonsilitis was transferred as diphtheria after 2 days stay – a bacteriological examination having been made.

Five cases in all of diphtheria were dealt with, but none of these cases were obvious contacts of previous cases.

Eight cases in all of mumps have been admitted & two of these were close contacts of the earlier cases the disease becoming apparent after 18 & 22 days respectively after date of last contact.

Two cases of Rubella have been admitted. Two cases of chicken pox, one of measles & one of whooping cough, & a case of suspected phthisis – which was never definitely diagnosed (no bacilli found in sputum) were also admitted.

One case of scabies was admitted as the associated impetigo was very severe

54 cases in all have passed through the A&D book & of these 31 were actually admitted to the Hospital.

Administrative

The Hospital was opened with a staff of 16 N.C.O.s & men
in detail. A Staff Sergt. (Nursing)
    Sergt. Compounder.
   6 Nursing orderlies
   2 Cooks
   2 Washermen
   4 General Duty orderlies.
with a Sergt & private Clerk & a pack store Keeper.

The washerman in excess was rendered necessary by an amount of soiled Hospital Material & clothing that had been brought from Saffron Walden

The General Duty orderly was used as the state of the Hospital when it was opened made a full & rapid cleaning imperative; & there were also builders labourers in the House for the 1st fortnight.

Two nursing orderlies were detailed for night work & were on duty from 8 p.m. to 7 a.m. — These received their main meal from the cooks about 9 p.m.

The day staff were on duty from 7 a.m. till 8 p.m. & each member of it received three hours off duty daily either between 10 a.m. & 1 p.m. or between 2 p.m. — 5 p.m. as I considered this necessary when the infectious nature of the diseases they were nursing was considered

The staff were billeted in a stable in the grounds which gave them ample room on a 40 foot basis per man after slight alterations had been made.

The Staff's Hospital were considered to be completely isolated from the rest of the Town & one of the cooks was generally sent for such medical comforts as were supplied by the A.S.C.

As the Hospital has never been full a large ward was given to the staff as a Barrack Room, to obviate crowding of the Kitchen which was the only other room available for them. This proved a satisfactory arrangement.

The Pack Store Keeper combined his duties with those of the Steward, which in such a small Hospital were not sufficient to keep him fully employed, also because he was under instructions

2/L London Field ambulance

War Diary.
Oct 1915.

Appendix I

"A" Form.
MESSAGES AND SIGNALS.
Army Form C. 2121.

No. of Message

Prefix	Code	m.	Words	Charge	This message is on a/c of:	Recd. at 6p m.
Office of Origin and Service Instructions			Sent At 1.20 p m. To By		Service. (Signature of "Franking Officer.")	Date From By

TO ~~2/6th R.F.A 2/7th R.F.A 2/14th BN~~
   ~~2/15th BN   2/4th F. AMB~~
   ~~2/16th BN~~

Sender's Number	Day of Month	In reply to Number	
S.C. 106	fourth		A A A

Operations finished Unit
proceed home independently

From 179th Inf Bde
Place
Time 1.15 pm

Signature: G. Blacker?
9/8 Major
175 Inf Bde

Appendix I

"A" Form.   Army Form C. 2121.
MESSAGES AND SIGNALS.   No. of Message

Prefix	Code	m.	Words	Charge	This message is on a/c of :	Recd. at 12·35p m.
Office of Origin and Service Instructions			Sent At m. To By		Service. (Signature of "Franking Officer.")	Date 11 x From Bde HQ By S.S.O.

TO ~~2/4th FA~~ 2/4th FN 2/6 RFA 2/4 F Amb.

Sender's Number: SC 105   Day of Month: Fourth   In reply to Number: AAA

Reports to Norman HO AAA are taking up position from ELSENHAM STA to B— BOLLINGTON HALL AAA 2/6th RFA will select position for guns to west of QUENDON STANSTED ROAD AAA 2/4th RFA is to E of same road

From: 179th Inf Bde
Place:
Time: 12.30

Signature: A Blaikie Capt
a/Staff Capt
179th Inf Bde

"A" Form.   Army Form C. 2121.

MESSAGES AND SIGNALS.

No. of Message

Prefix	Code	m.	Words	Charge	This message is on a/c of:	Recd. at	m.
Office of Origin and Service Instructions.			Sent			Date	
			At	m.	Service.	From	
			To				
			By		(Signature of "Franking Officer.")	By	

TO   O/C   2/4   London   F Amb
INN N of ORFORD HOUSE

Sender's Number	Day of Month	In reply to Number		AAA
MCII	4/11/15	MC 56.		

I Have established Dressing Station in Empty House cross roads EAST of last I in STANSTED MOUNT-FITCH ET aaa Tel no. 31 STANSTED aaa II at 12.45pm sent forward Captain SPENCER with five Horse Ambulances and bearers. I have instructed him to immediately report to you position of his Wagon Rendez-vous. aaa. message ends.

From O/C Dressing Station
Place Cross Roads STANSTED MOUNT FITCHET
Time 1.25 pm

The above may be forwarded as now corrected.   (Z)

Censor.   Signature of Addressee or person authorized to telegraph in his name

* This line should be erased if not required.

8350 S. B. Ltd. Wt. W4843/541—50,000. 9/14. Forms C2121/10.

"A" Form. Army Form C. 2121.
MESSAGES AND SIGNALS.

TO: 2/4 LONDON FIELD AMBᶜᵉ

Sender's Number: M.C.54
Day of Month: 4.XI.15.
AAA

our advanced guard in touch
with enemy scouts at QUENDON
aaa nothing further at present
aaa

mounted orderly
by Sergt Stephens

From: OC 2/4 Lond F Amb
Place: INN S. of QUENDON.
Time: 11.14 4.XI.15.

"A" Form.
MESSAGES AND SIGNALS.
Army Form C. 2121.

TO: 2/4 LONDON FIELD AMBCE

Sender's Number: Mc.55
Day of Month: 5.X.15

Brigade is retiring to S of ORFORD HOUSE aaa if necessary retire yourself conforming to the rear destiny of artillery aaa

by cyclist orderly

From: OC 2/4 Lond Fld Ambce
Place: INN S of QUENDON
Time: 12.10

"A" Form.   Army Form C. 2121.
MESSAGES AND SIGNALS.

Sender's Number	Day of Month	In reply to Number		
M.C. 56	4.XI.15			AAA

Bde is taking up a position ELSENHAM STA B of BOLLINGTON HQ. aaa Bn HQ. N of NORMAN HO aaa prepare dressing station in STANSTEAD aaa unpack nothing aaa send forward bearers and inform me of position of wagon rendezvous aaa massage aaa

From OC. 2/4 London Field Amb
Place INN N. of ORFORD HO.
Time 12.35

"A" Form.   Army Form C. 2121.

MESSAGES AND SIGNALS.

Prefix	Code	m.	Words	Charge	This message is on a/c of:	Recd. at m.
Office of Origin and Service Instructions			Sent			Date
			At m.		Service.	From
			To			
			By		(Signature of "Franking Officer.")	By

TO { 2/4 LONDON FIELD AMB ce

| Sender's Number | Day of Month | In reply to Number | |
| * M.C. 57 | 6.XI.15 | | AAA |

operations finished area go home

From O.C. 2/4 London Field Amb
Place 12.46.
Time   N.A.KURMAN 140

Signature JB Taylor

The above arrangements proved satisfactory & ran smoothly after the first few days.

G R Pritchard
Capt.
RAMC
2/4 Lond. F Amb'ce

The charge of the Hospital was transferred to
Capt. Spencer on the 17th Dec. 1915.
  There were 8 men in Hospital.
    Mumps 3. Varicella 2. Bromidrosis 1. Impetigo 1.
From 17th to 25th Decr.
  further cases were admitted for treatment at this
    Hospital.
      Facial Cellulitis   1
      Sycosis   1
      Varicella   1
      Tinea circinata   1
      Mumps   1
  During this period a case of Diphtheria had
    been admitted for transference to the Civil Fever Hospl.
  and a case of Gonorrhoea for transference to Barnwell
    Military Hospl.
  A case of Varicella had been found free of infection
    and given sick leave being discharged from Hospital.
  On the 25th Dec, there were 11 cases of Infectious disease
    in Hospital for treatment.
All the cases above mentioned, treated in this Hospital,
  were of a mild nature; there were no complications
  or untoward signs or symptoms.
Dec. 28. There were no further admissions of mumps

Dec. 28 or Varicella, but a case of Seborrhoea Sicca was admitted on the 27th for treatment.

The charge of Hospital was handed over to Capt. Nash on the 29th am.

A. R. Spencer.
Capt. R.A.M.C.

Report of M.O. i/c Reception Hospital.
2/4th San. Fld. Ambulance.
Bishops Stortford.
31. 12. 1915.

Diary by Captn. Nash.

I took over the Reception Hospital on the evening of 28:12:15.

1. <u>Medical</u>.

There were 12 cases in Hospital:—
Mumps 4.   Chicken Pox 2.   Tinea 2.
Impetigo 1.   Facial Cellulitis 1.   Sycosis 1.
Seborrhoea Sicca 1.

On the 30th admitted one case of Mumps from 2/16th Battn. London Regt.

31st   Admitted a case of mumps from 2/4th San. Fld. Ambce. This man was undergoing segregation as a case had occurred in a child at his billet on 16/12/15.

2. <u>Administrative</u>.

The Staff consists of:—
1. Sergt. Dispenser.   2. Sergt. Nursing Orderlies. 4 day orderlies.   2 night orderlies.   3 general orderlies.
2 cook.   2 washer men.
15 of the above are billeted in Hospital.
1 Sergt. Clerk. 1 private clerk)   1 assistant dispenser.
[1 corporal Pack Storekeeper] (attends daily from 8.30 am to 6 pm)
(attends daily at intervals

The day staff come on duty at 7. am. & are relieved at 8 pm. by night orderlies who carry on until 7am. Each of day staff has 3 hours off duty, either morning or afternoon.

2.

	Patients	Staff
Breakfasts	7.45. a.m.	8. a.m.
Dinner.	12.45. p.m.	1. p.m.
Tea.	4.45. p.m.	5. p.m.
Supper.		7.30. p.m.

<u>Sanitary</u>

One bath available for patients of which the heating arrangements are not very satisfactory.

The Staff use the same bath after being thoroughly disinfected.

There are 2 water closets in use, one for Staff & one for patients. The W.C. in use by Staff has a leak in chamber which has been reported.

One night latrine for staff.

The Sergt. Dispenser & Sergt. Nursing Orderly sleep in the precincts of the hospital.

The remainder of Staff sleep in a loft over detached coach house.

Blankets of personnell have all just undergone disinfection.

All patients & Staff use a antiseptic mouth wash daily several times.

Geo Nash. Capt. R.A.M.C.T.
M/O i.c. Hospital 2/4 Hssr

www.ingramcontent.com/pod-product-compliance
Lightning Source LLC
Chambersburg PA
CBHW081459160426
43193CB00013B/2540